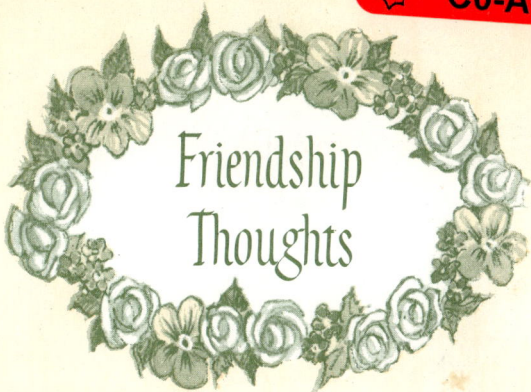

Friendship Thoughts

Friendship is the sunshine
That turns the sky to gold.
Friendship is the fragrance
A thousand blessings hold.

*Friendship is the pathway that
Leads to dreams come true . . .
For friendship is the blessing
Of knowing someone like you.*

from *Your friend — Diann*

Author Unknown

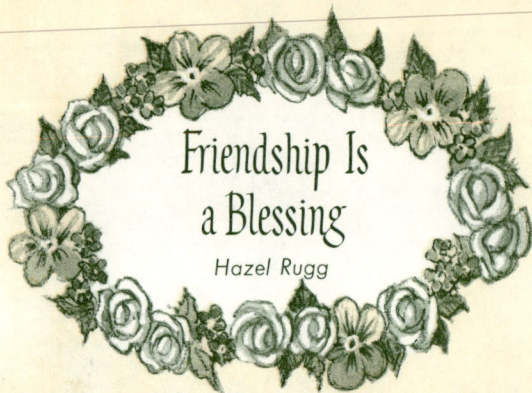

Friendship Is a Blessing

Hazel Rugg

God gives us many wondrous things,
I see them day by day . . .
The grass, the trees, the sky above
And flowers by the way.
The sun so warm, the moon of gold
And stars up in the sky
All speak together of the love
Of Him who dwells on high.

But greater far than these are friends
He gives us on life's way,
Whose fellowship gives help and strength
And courage day by day.
I'm thankful for each one of mine
And pray that I can be
The loving, trusting, helpful friend
That each has been to me.

Friendship Is a Lovely Thing

Evelyn Keller

In all the world there is
   no lovelier thing than friendship . . .

It's like a breath of early spring
   that makes the day so fair;
It's like the cool soft wind that blows
   to chase away each care.

It's like the sunshine ushering in
   a new and brighter day . . .
It's like the shining morning star
   that draws the night away.

It's God's own gift to everyone
   to treasure and to hold . . .
So guard and tend it lovingly,
   it's worth far more than gold.

In all the world there is
   no lovelier thing than friendship.

Friendship Is a Lamp

Margaret Cameron

We lit the lamp of friendship
So many years ago,
And still it's burning brightly
Amid time's ebb and flow.

A beacon in the darkness
That cannot dim nor fade;
A light that will not falter
In sunshine or in shade.

As on life's road we travel,
Its friendly flame we see . . .
And may its light keep shining
Through all the years to be.

©

Friendship Is a Road

Garnett Ann Schultz

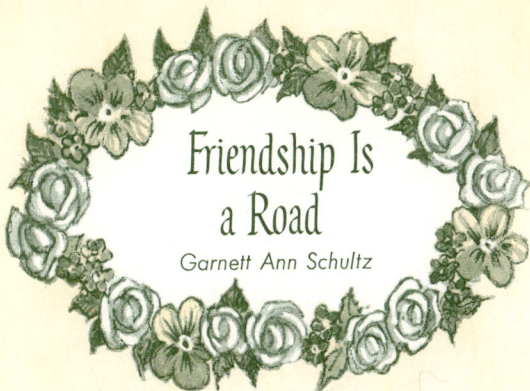

Along life's road I found a friend
Who brought me joys untold;
A happiness to fill my heart
More valuable than gold;

Along life's road, I found a smile,
And oh, my heart was glad,
For it was quite the sweetest one
That I had ever had . . .

Along life's road I found a faith
To fill my every day,
A trust in God, a hope anew
To ever mark my way;

A dream of bigger things to come,
A friend, a faith, a smile . . .
Along life's road, I found them all
To make my life worthwhile.

Friendship Is a Golden Chain

Vera Hardman

Friendship is a golden chain
Made stronger with each year;
Each link is forged of memories
That make you still more dear.

The thoughtful things you say and do
Become the links of gold
That I will treasure through the years
And in my heart will hold.

And always as I think of you,
It becomes a special day;
I'm glad my heart is linked to yours
In friendship's golden way.

Friendship Is a Key

Virginia Katherine Oliver

A smile is a key to friendship,
  One that is certain to fit
Right in the lock of every heart
  And open the door to it.

A kind deed is a special key;
  And when this one has been tried,
It seems to be the master key
  For the door swings open wide.

Often a word is just the key
  That will prove to be the best,
For the right word may open the lock
  Which is stronger than the rest.

Friendship's chain holds many a key,
  But each will ever depend
On care we take in the choice we make
  Of the key that gains a friend.

Friendship Is a Melody

Gladys Naomi Arnold

The friendships we treasure are those that
   have lasted
Through changes that come with the years;
When the leaves shed the lush green
   of springtime,
A deep golden color appears.

The warm glow of friendship enriches
   our lives
When faith with sincerity blends.
The music flows smoothly through distance
   and time . . .
The melody never ends.

Friendship Is
a Memory

Eva Rodes Orloff

Memories can be such beautiful things,
Frail, ethereal as butterflies' wings;
Bits of bright jewels, part of you and me.
Built of our thoughts so lovely and free;

Each one a blessing deep in the heart,
Each in experience having its start,
For friendship's a diamond, like a glimmering star
That shines through the darkness wherever you are.

It fills the gray corners with life's golden dreams
And leaves the soul brilliant in lovelier sheens.
Life can hold nothing more beautiful, fair,
Than friendship's sweet memories lingering there.

©

Friendship Is a Recipe

Mona K. Guldswog

Take a heap of joy, blend well with trust,
And a measure of dreams to share;
Add minds more than willing to understand
And hearts more than ready to care.
Fold in a generous fluff of forgiving nature,
Kindly word and thoughtful deed,
Then a pinch of humor and a dash of spice
Whipped in with loving speed.

A recipe as old as time itself
Yet always delightfully new . . .
They call it simply friendship,
Beloved, tried, and true.

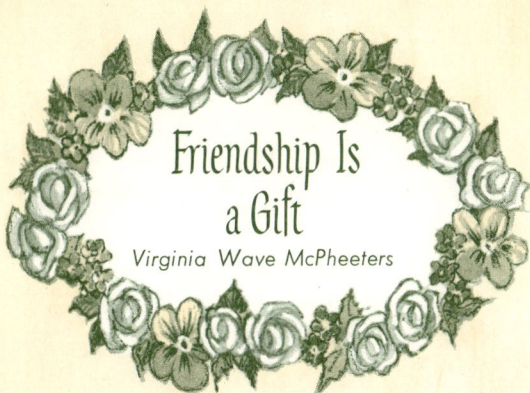

Friendship Is a Gift

Virginia Wave McPheeters

There is a beauty in the earth,
The mountains high, the valleys green,
The rippling brook, the waterfall,
The wild sweet rose so oft unseen . . .

The song of birds, the smell of spring,
Autumn colors bright and gay . . .
A thousand treasures we can find
If we but look about each day.

Yes, gracious is the bounty
That God to man does send;
Then as a crowning glory
God gave to man . . . a friend.

Friendship Is a Ship

Pollyanna Sedziol

Friendship is a blessed ship,
It sails both calm and storm;
It weathers well, its course is true,
It makes the heart grow warm.

Its crew is love and joy and good,
Kindness, mercy, smiles and cheer;
It sails quite boldly everywhere
Casting out dividing fear.

It's launched and blessed by God above
Who fills His children with His love;
It's nourished by dear kindly thoughts . . .
Good deeds are often by it wrought.

No greater boon to man than this . . .
Bright hours within sweet friendship's bliss;
No better days than those well spent
With friends in whom we are content.

Friendship Is
Love

Bess Meredith

Friendship is love and mutual faith,
Receiving, sharing too;
Never demanding, just understanding . . .
Comforting, tender and true.

Friendship is a gentle, fragile thing,
Yet tenuous and strong.
It stretches out and reaches far
And lasts a whole life long.

And when the light of friendship shines
On rain in clouds nearby,
Then lovely bands of color arch
A rainbow in life's sky.

Friendship Is a Garden

Patience Strong

Scatter seeds of friendship, thoughts and
words and deeds . . . Though the soil looks
stony, scatter wide your seeds. Every
kindly action, every word sincere . . . Every
good intention meant to help and cheer is
a seed of friendship . . . And somewhere, someday,
it will bud and blossom in its own sweet way.

*Time must bring its changes as the years roll
by . . . Flowers of love must perish, friendships
fade and die. But if you have scattered all
along the track, seeds of true affection . . .
You will never lack. Always there'll be
someone who will understand . . . Someone who is
ready with a helping hand. Do not dread the
future, full of doubts and fears . . . Sow the
seeds of friendship for the coming years.*

©

Friendship Is a Smile

LaVerne P. Larson

A happy friendly smile
Is a tonic you will find,
If you see one or you wear one
You can leave your cares behind.

It can work a bit of magic
Everywhere you go,
It's like a seed of happiness
That always seems to grow.

You can give away a smile
And the minute that you do,
Another heart will gladly
Send one back to you.

Smiles are like sunbeams
Bringing warmth and special cheer
To all the folks around us
Through every passing year.

Friendship Is Eternal

Catherine Plumb

Friendship is like a song . . .
A beautiful melody that lingers on.

Friendship is like a ray of light . . .
Its radiance is pure and bright.

Friendship is like a flower . . .
Its beauty has infinite power.

Friendship is like a star . . .
That guides the way, near and far.

Friendship is like a prayer . . .
Its benediction is always there.